Ollie Finds a New Home

The Story of a Burrowing Owl on Marco Island

Roseanne Pawelec

Illustrated by Sue Lynn Cotton

the Peppertree Press

Sarasota, Florida

For information regarding permission,
call 941-922-2662 or contact us at our website:
www.peppertreepublishing.com or write to:
the Peppertree Press, LLC.
Attention: Publisher
1269 First Street, Suite 7
Sarasota, Florida 34236

ISBN: 978-1-61493-383-0

Library of Congress Number: 2015911294

Printed August 2015

For JoJo and Alex.

Thank you for asking me to tell you a story.

Nancy and Bob Burrows made their home on a vacant sandy lot with a view down the mouth of a long canal on Marco Island. Last spring, the happy couple welcomed two new additions to their family, their newborn burrowing owls, Ollie and Nettie.

During the days that followed, Mom and Dad watched as their babies grew, thriving in the warmth and in the sunshine. Little Ollie, in particular, would look forward to days outside with his Dad. He would swing from his wooden T-perch and show off for his father now that he could fly. "Look at me Dad," Ollie would shout. "See how high I can fly? Watch this Dad. Bet I could beat you in a race."

Ollie also kept busy during the day helping his sister. He was teaching Nettie to fly, just as his Dad had taught him.

"Now Nettie, there's a trick Dad taught me. Look. We can flap our wings and stay like this in mid-air. Dad says it's called "hovering." You can do it too Nettie. Give it a try."

With Ollie's support and encouragement, Nettie improved every day. Ollie was sure Nettie would be able to fly by her 6th week birthday, now just 1 week away.

Ollie enjoyed this routine. He was one happy burrowing owl. At least he was, until his Dad called a meeting of his family that evening. He told everyone to gather at 5:30 p.m. in the kitchen on the lowest level of Ollie's home, about 5 feet underground in the burrow.

"Dad, what's the meeting all about? asked Ollie.

"I'll tell you tonight son. Be patient," Dad said.

Before the meeting, Ollie followed the long, dark twisty hallway of his family's burrow to his bedroom, and did what he did every day at 5 o'clock. He took down the special box from his closet which held his most prized possessions. Ollie opened the lid and looked inside. There was the piece of shell from the egg Ollie hatched from. His Mom had given it to him. He remembered Mom telling him, "This is to mark the day you were born, Ollie." Next to the piece of shell, there was a long brown spotted feather which came from Great Grandmother Athene. It was so soft. But Ollie's favorite treasure was an old weathered piece of driftwood. It was part of Dad's first T-perch when his Dad was a little owl.

Ollie carefully put each item back into the box and headed for the kitchen for the important meeting. He took his seat at the kitchen table next to Nettie.

"I'm afraid I have some bad news, Ollie and Nettie. We have to move in a few short weeks. The developer who bought the land upstairs is starting construction on a house. We can't stay here. We are being re-homed," said Dad.

"Re-homed, what does that mean?" said Little Ollie. He was getting more and more upset. He started chirping and chattering. He kept bobbing his head.

"Calm down Ollie," Dad urged. "Your mother and I will find a new home, even better than this one."

"But why do we have to move," cried Ollie. "I like it here. I don't want to move."

"Well son, we don't have a choice," explained Ollie's Dad. "The man who bought this piece of property can start construction on a new house for his own family. Under the law in Marco Island, we can stay here up until there are no eggs in the nest or the youngest can fly. When Nettie learns to fly, we can be re-homed at another burrow nearby."

"It just isn't fair Dad," cried Ollie. He knew he would miss this home. He was born here and learned to fly here, his biggest accomplishment. He could see the water from his perch. The neighborhood was so quiet.

The very next day Mom and Dad took Ollie and Nettie to see some nearby burrows on the Island. At the first stop, the Realtor, Dave Hoots, was describing the most attractive features of the first burrow they saw.

"This home is very spacious," Realtor Dave explained. "It's a full eight feet underground. There's plenty of room to make it your own."

But Ollie didn't like this home. The T-perch wasn't in the sunshine, and you couldn't see the water. The street was busy with cars racing past it. Most importantly, it wasn't home. His Dad asked him what he thought. "Look at how big your room would be," Dad said.

Ollie didn't want to disappoint his Dad so he said nothing and just smiled.

Realtor Dave showed the Burrows two more homes that day, each one bigger than the last. "Most homes for burrowing owls are 1 to 4 feet underground," said Mr. Hoots. "The homes you saw today are all a full 7 to 8 feet underground. They're hard to find," he emphasized.

The Burrows agreed to meet Realtor Dave in the morning to look at a few more homes, and returned to their own burrow that evening with a sad looking Ollie in tow.

His Dad decided to have a talk with him after dinner. Mom had made some of Ollie's favorite foods, grilled grasshoppers and pickled beetles, but Ollie simply wasn't hungry.

"Ollie, I know how hard this move is on you son. But I want you to think about some good things which will come from the change. You'll meet new friends, owls your own age who enjoy doing the same things you do. You may get your own room, and not have to share a room with your sister anymore. Your mom may have more moms to talk to, and would be happier too. Many good things can come from change son. You simply need to open those big round eyes of yours to see the possibilities."

Ollie thought hard about what his Dad had said. In the morning, the family was off with Realtor Hoots again to see another burrow.

This one was different, according to Mr. Hoots. It was in a gated community for burrowing owls called The Colony. It certainly looked different to Ollie. The rope and stick fencing around the burrows took up most of the lot. There were owls sitting on their T-perches everywhere. There were Moms and Dads and lots of owls who looked to be his age. The Colony was on a nice level lot. You couldn't see the water, but still, the owls there looked like they were having fun. Many of them were posing for pictures. There were tourists with cameras. "It might be fun to get my picture in the paper," Ollie thought to himself.

As Realtor Dave showed them through the burrow and heard his Mom commenting on the brand new kitchen, one of the owls he saw playing outside came up to him. "Hi, my name's Henry," he said. "Are you moving here? If you are, we could use you on our soccer team. We're an owl short," Henry explained. Ollie didn't know what to say. "It's up to my Mom and Dad," he said.

When the tour of the burrow was finished, Ollie's Mom and Dad told Realtor Hoots that this was the home they liked best. They asked him how soon they could move in.

That weekend, the Burrows Family held a birthday celebration for 6 week old Nettie.

She blew out the candles on her Chocolate Mouse cake, then she and Ollie headed outside. Ollie told his Mom and Dad to take their seats on the double T-perch. "Mom and Dad," Ollie proudly proclaimed, "I present the Flying Nettie." With that, Nettie took flight from her perch, swooping up and down around her parents and her brother and hovered in mid-air just as Ollie had taught her.

"Good job Nettie," said Mom and Dad. "You too son," Dad added. "You did a great job teaching your sister."

When the celebration was over, Ollie joined his Dad in taking some of his family's belongings over to their new burrow in The Colony.

In one of the big cartons Ollie carried was his special treasures box. Ollie put the box in his new bedroom. He opened the lid and looked inside. There was the hatched shell piece and the feather and the section of Dad's childhood T-perch. Ollie decided to add one new treasure to his box. He carefully placed a piece of his own T-perch inside. It had come from the only home Ollie had ever known, up until today.

"Someday when I grow up and have a family I will give this to my own little owl," Ollie said out loud. Then Ollie raced from his bedroom to find his father. "Dad," Ollie called. "Can I go out and play?"

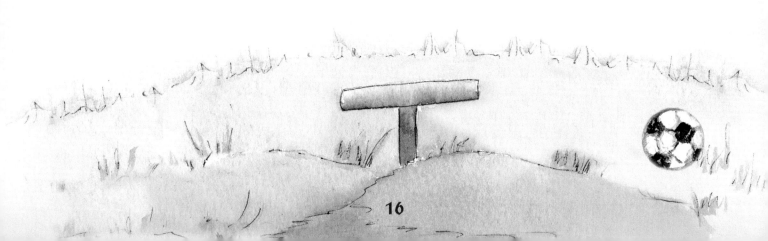

Reader's Exercise

Now that you've read "Ollie Finds a New Home in Marco Island,"
let's find out how much you've learned about Burrowing Owls.
See if you can correctly answer the questions below.

1.) Where do burrowing owls live?

      a. In the sky.

      b. In the ocean

      c. In the ground

2.) What do burrowing owls do when they're upset?

      a. Bite.

      b. Bob their heads and chirp.

      c. Spread their wings and fly.

3.) When do burrowing owls learn to fly?

      a. At 6 months old.

      b. At 6 years old.

      c. At 6 weeks old.

4.) What do burrowing owls eat?

      a. Insects and mice

      b. Grass and Leaves

      c. Macaroni and Cheese

5.) What can burrowing owls do when they hunt for food?

      a.) Hover in mid-air.

      b.) Somersault backwards.

      c.) Stand on their heads.

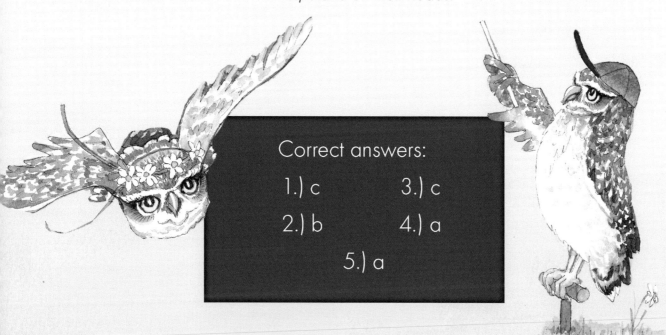

Correct answers:

1.) c   3.) c

2.) b   4.) a

5.) a

CPSIA information can be obtained
at www.ICGtesting.com
Printed in the USA
LVIC06n0223040316
477731LV00002B/8